Watch It Grow
Snake
Barrie Watts

W
FRANKLIN WATTS
LONDON • SYDNEY

This edition 2005

First published in 2002 by Franklin Watts
96 Leonard Street, London EC2A 4XD

Franklin Watts Australia
45-51 Huntley Street, Alexandria, NSW 2015

© Barrie Watts 2002

Editor: Adrian Cole
Art director: Jonathan Hair
Photographer: Barrie Watts
Illustrator: David Burroughs
Consultant: Beverley Mathias, REACH

A CIP catalogue record for this book
is available from the British Library

ISBN 0 7496 6122 4

Dewey Classification 594

Printed in Hong Kong, China

Picture credits: page 28, Geoff Trinder/Ardea London

How to use this book

Watch It Grow has been specially designed to cater for a range of reading and learning abilities. Initially children may just follow the pictures. Ask them to describe in their own words what they see. Other children will enjoy reading the single sentence in large type, in conjunction with the pictures. This single sentence is then expanded in the main text. More adept readers will be able to follow the text and pictures by themselves through to the conclusion of the life cycle. **Please note:** a Carolina corn snake (Elaphe guttata) was used as the subject for this book, and does not reflect the growth or behaviour of all types of snake.

Contents

Snakes come from eggs. 4

The baby snake grows inside. 6

The snake hatches. 8

The baby snake looks after itself. 10

The baby snake has its first meal. 12

The snake sheds its skin. 14

The snake changes its skin colour. 16

The snake can move quickly. 18

The snake basks in the sun. 20

The snake hunts for food. 22

The snake catches a meal. 24

The snake sleeps through the winter. 26

The female snake lays her eggs. 28

Word bank 30

Life cycle 31

Index 32

Snakes come from eggs.

Snake eggs are about
25 millimetres long and have a
soft, leathery shell. Inside each
one a baby snake is growing.
A female snake lays her eggs
in the spring. She may lay as
many as 20 eggs.

The eggs are laid in a hole in damp soil. The soil keeps the eggs warm so the baby snakes can grow.

The baby snake grows inside.

The eggs take about 10 weeks to
hatch. Inside the egg, the baby
snake feeds off the egg yolk.
This helps it to grow strong.

The baby snake breathes air through tiny holes in the egg shell. When it is ready to hatch, the snake cuts through the tough shell with its **egg tooth**.

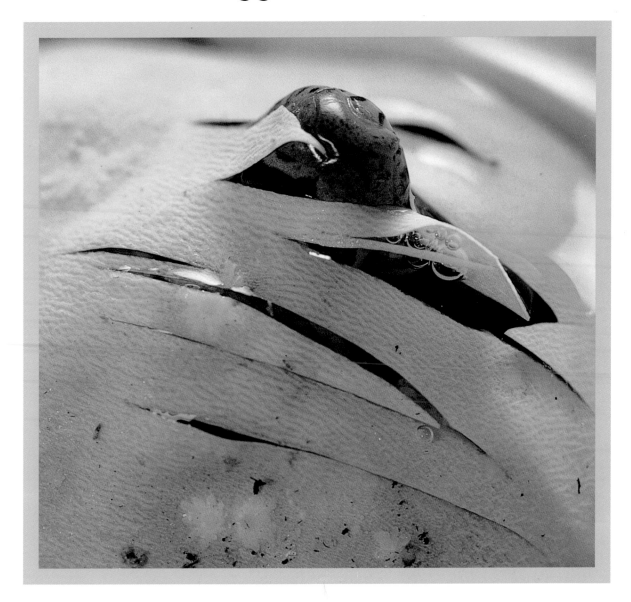

The snake hatches.

The snake pushes its head out of the egg. It looks like its parents, but is a different colour and is much smaller in size.

When the snake hatches it is only as big as a pencil. By the time it is fully grown, it can be over 2 metres long.

The baby snake looks after itself.

The snake can swim and climb as soon as it hatches.

It must catch its own food and keep away from **predators**.
It has to be very careful as some birds, mammals and even other snakes would like to eat it.

The baby snake has its first meal.

Two or three days after
hatching, the baby snake
begins looking for food.
It usually waits until it is dark.

The baby snake mainly eats animals that are slow-moving and easy to catch. It often eats young birds and mice that are still in their nest.

The snake sheds its skin.

Two weeks after hatching the young
snake has grown too big for its old skin.
A new skin grows under the old one.

The snake turns a dull colour
and its eyes become cloudy.
It is ready to **moult**.
The snake rubs itself against a
rough stone. This helps it wriggle
out of the old
skin, which it
then leaves
behind.

The snake
will moult
many times
again during
its life.

The snake changes its skin colour.

The colour of the snake's skin changes each time it **moults**. The skin becomes more colourful as the snake grows older.

Once it is fully grown, this snake will have brown skin with red patches on it. These colours help to **camouflage** the snake from its **predators**.

The snake lives on sandy
ground among leaves,
rocks and fallen branches.
It can hide very easily.

The snake can move quickly.

After five months the snake has doubled in size. It has a long backbone made up of over 200 small bones. The joints are stretchy and bendy.

The snake can race over the ground by using its powerful muscles in an 'S' movement. It grips the ground with its belly **scales**. It can move faster than you can run.

The snake basks in the sun.

The snake, like all **reptiles**, is cold-blooded. Its blood temperature changes with hot or cold weather. If the snake is cold, it cannot move quickly enough to catch food.

The snake must warm itself by **basking** in the sun. Its **scales** stop it from drying out. When the snake is warm enough, it looks for food.

The snake hunts for food.

The snake does not have good eyesight, but it does have a good sense of smell. Its forked tongue picks up scents and carries them to a special sense organ in the snake's mouth, called **Jacobson's Organ**.

When the snake hunts it uses its tongue to follow the scent trails left behind by its **prey**.

The snake catches a meal.

The snake uses its teeth to catch its **prey**. It has caught a large mouse. The snake then coils its body around the prey and kills it by **constriction**.

The snake cannot chew its prey. Instead, it uses powerful throat and jaw muscles to swallow it whole, head first.

The snake sleeps through the winter.

After seven months, as winter approaches, the snake finds a place to **hibernate**. It looks for a hollow in a tree or a hole under a rock. It must sleep through the winter in order to survive the cold.

During hibernation the snake's heartbeat slows down and its blood temperature becomes colder. It uses its body fat as food to stay alive.

The female snake lays her eggs.

In early spring the snake emerges from **hibernation**. It spends a few days **basking** in the sun. An adult male snake uses his sense of smell to find a female and mates with her. Soon after mating the female snake lays her eggs.

The female snake makes a hole in warm, damp soil and one by one pushes the eggs out of an opening in her body. She may lay some more later in a different place. When she has laid her eggs, she leaves the baby snakes to hatch by themselves.

Word bank

Basking - when a snake lies in the sun to warm up its cold blood so it can move around quickly.

Camouflage - when the colour and pattern of an animal's skin is similar to its surroundings, so it is hard to see. Camouflage helps an animal to hide.

Constriction - when a snake coils its body around an animal and squeezes it to stop it breathing.

Egg tooth - a small tooth used by a baby snake to break through the shell of its egg. It disappears shortly after birth.

Hibernate - when an animal hides away and goes into a deep sleep for the winter while the weather is cold.

Jacobson's Organ - this is found on the roof of a snake's mouth and helps it to sense smells.

Moult - when a snake sheds its skin.

Predators - meat-eating animals. Snake's predators include some birds, mammals and even other snakes.

Prey - any animal that is hunted for food by another animal.

Reptiles - the group of scaly, cold-blooded animals which include snakes, crocodiles and tortoises.

Scales - these small, hard plates cover the whole of a snake's body.

Life cycle

Ten weeks after the eggs are laid, the baby snake hatches.

In early spring, after mating, an adult female snake lays her own eggs.

The baby snake can swim and climb. It must look after itself.

When winter approaches, the snake hibernates.

Two weeks after hatching, the snake sheds its skin for the first time.

The snake kills its prey by constriction and then swallows it whole.

The snake's skin colour changes as it gets older. Its colour helps it hide.

After five months the snake has doubled in size. It moves quickly using its belly scales.

Index

basking 21, 28

camouflage 16
constriction 25

egg *or* eggs 4, 5, 6, 7, 8, 28, 29
egg tooth 7

food 10, 12, 20, 21, 26

hatch, hatches *or* hatching 6, 7, 8, 9, 10, 12, 14, 29
hibernate *or* hibernation 26, 28

Jacobson's Organ 22

mate *or* mating 28
moult *or* moults 15, 16

scales 19, 21
sense of smell 22, 28
skin 14, 15
    colour 8, 15, 16

yolk 6